FranklinCovey™

# Loving ♥ Reminders

## for couples

60 affectionate notes & stickers
for those close to your heart.

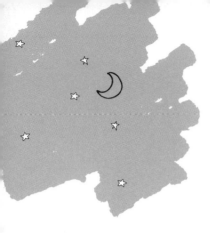

**Also available, *Loving Reminders for kids.***

*Special Acknowledgments:*

*Conceived and developed by Cheryl Kerzner*
*Designed and illustrated by Kim Mann*
*Written by Emme Griffith*

**S**o often, as I've lectured and taught around the world, couples have told me about their need to find ways to connect with each other. Too easily, we slip into a pattern of mundane existence. If relations with our loved one are healthy, it's easier to go onto the next daily routine or task.

In my book, *The 7 Habits of Highly Effective Families,* I use the metaphor of the Emotional Bank Account to represent the quality of the relationship you have with others. It's like a financial bank account in that you can make "deposits" by doing positive things that build trust. A high balance in your Emotional Bank Account represents a high level of trust with your loved one. Communication is open and free. But if the account balance is low or overdrawn, there is no authentic communication. The balance of trust in the account determines how well you can communicate and solve problems with another person.

Hopefully, this book of messages will become one more opportunity for you to make a "deposit" in your own relationship. No matter what the situation, there are always things you can do that will make relationships better. Everyone deserves a little *Loving Reminder.*

 *Stephen R. Covey*

# ◎ Turn these pages
# into Loving Reminders.

- Simply remove a message from the book.

- Write in a personal good wish.

• Fold as shown.

• Seal with a sticker from the back of the book.

• Tuck your *Loving Reminder* in a clever spot.

# Loving Reminders
# for couples

i love you

Life is
good!

you're very special to me

# Thinking of you...

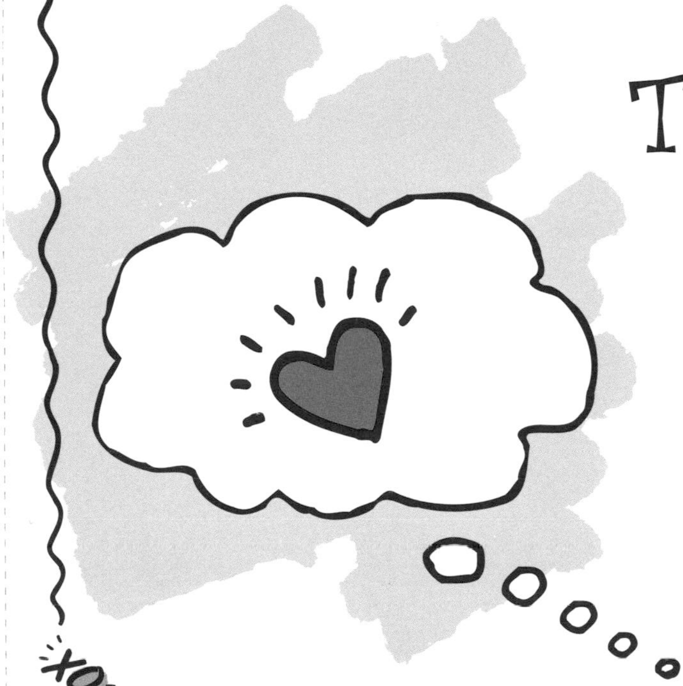

Forever,
& ever & ever.

have a great trip

# Pack up a few thoughts of me!

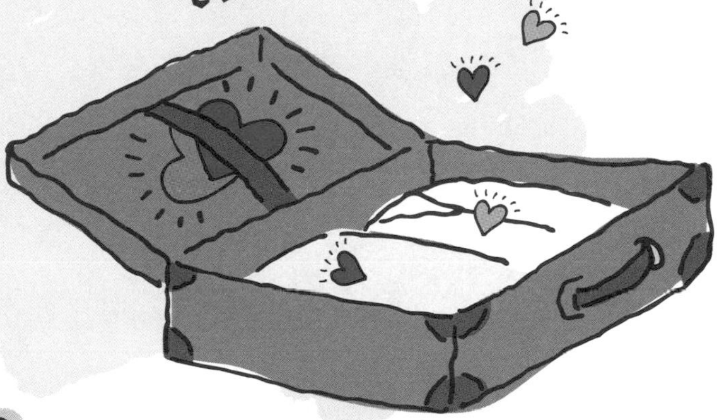

i love you

You mean so much to me.

**h o n e y - d o   l i s t :**

1. _____

2. _____

3. Give me a big kiss.

let's talk . . .

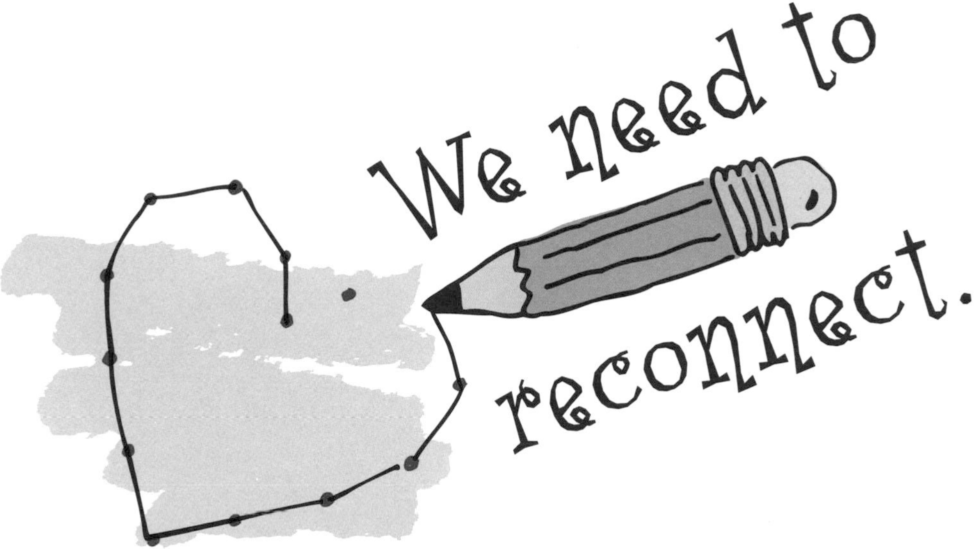

i'm sorry

Let's mend fences.

I'm glad
I found you.

feel better soon

There's a hug
tucked in
here!

Thanks for
being there
for me.

good luck

With love,
from your #1 fan!

missing you

# I just blew you a kiss!

i love you

Life is
good!

you're very special to me

# Thinking of you...

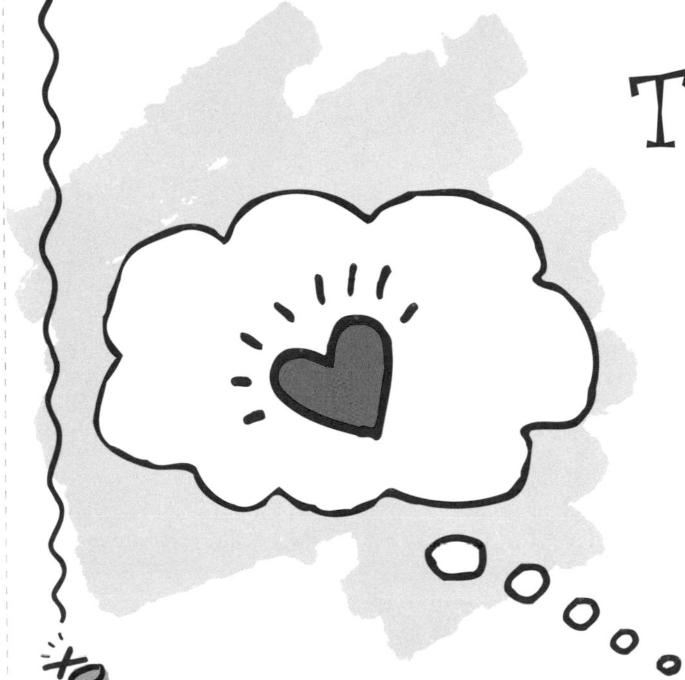

have a great trip

Pack up a few thoughts of me!

let's talk...

We need to reconnect.

you have everything it takes...

And then some!

i'm sorry

Let's mend fences.

how did i get so lucky?

# I'm glad I found you.

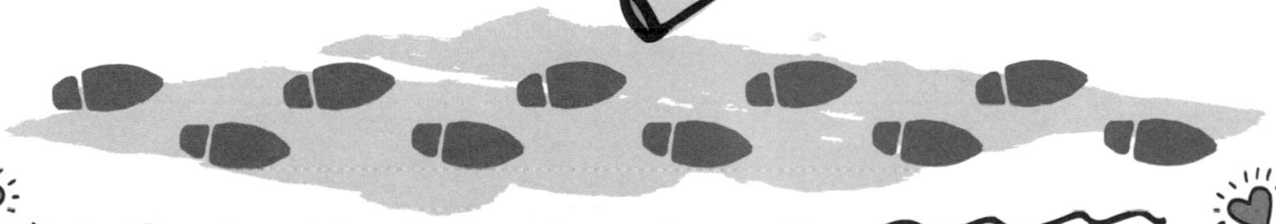

**how's this sound?**

Meet me at _____ for

a little _____

from _____ till _____ !

feel better soon

There's a hug
tucked in
here!

Thanks for
being there
for me.

you're the best!

Thanks for

_____ !

good luck

With love,
from your #1 fan!

missing you

# I just blew you a kiss!

# Life is good!

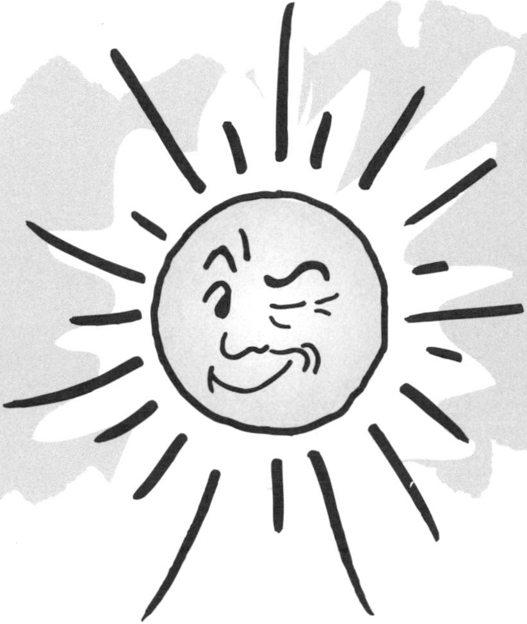

let's have some fun!

Tonight I'm going to

!

you're very special to me

# Thinking of you...

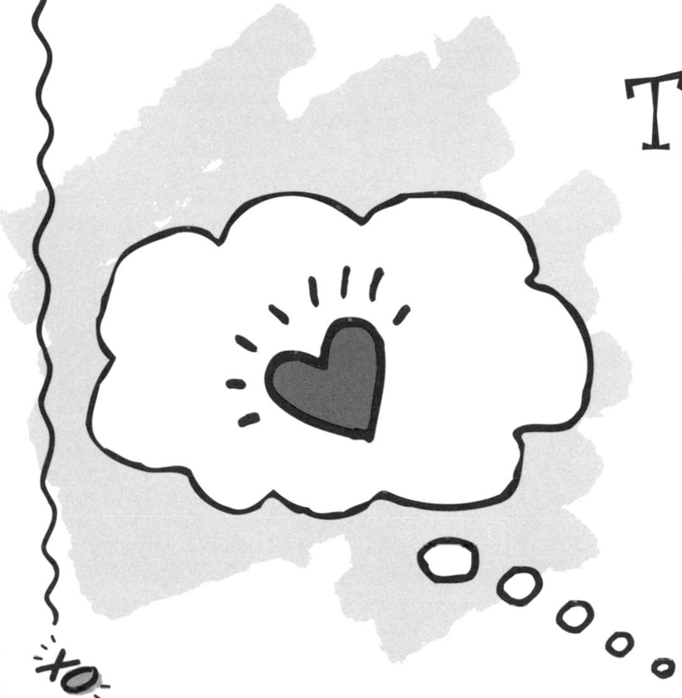

i ' m   h e r e   f o r   y o u . . .

# Forever,
# & ever & ever.

# Pack up a few thoughts of me!

honey-do list:

1. _____

2. _____

3. Give me a big kiss.

## let's talk . . .

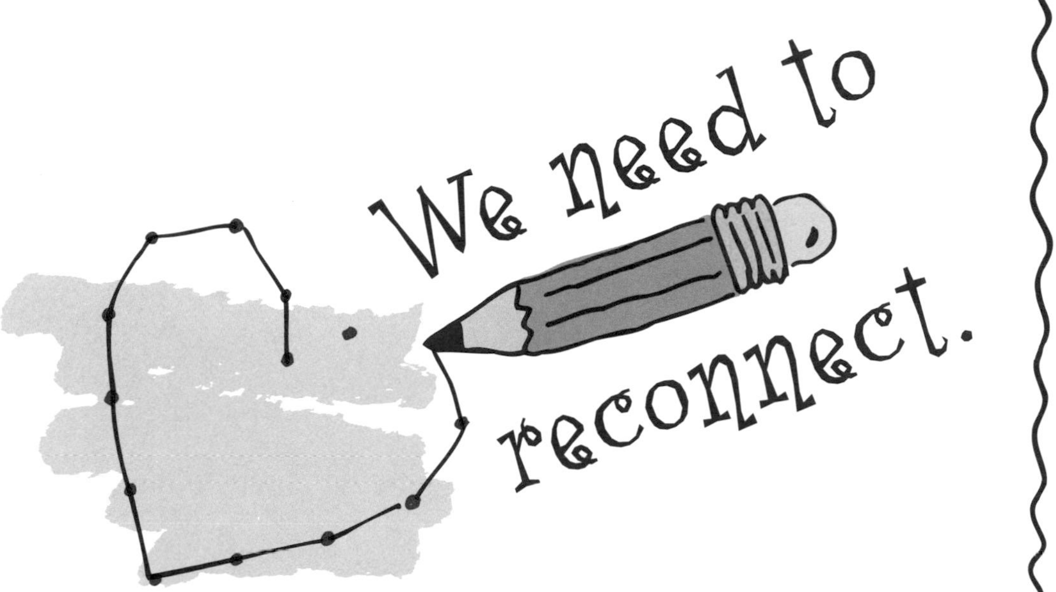

i'm sorry

# Let's mend fences.

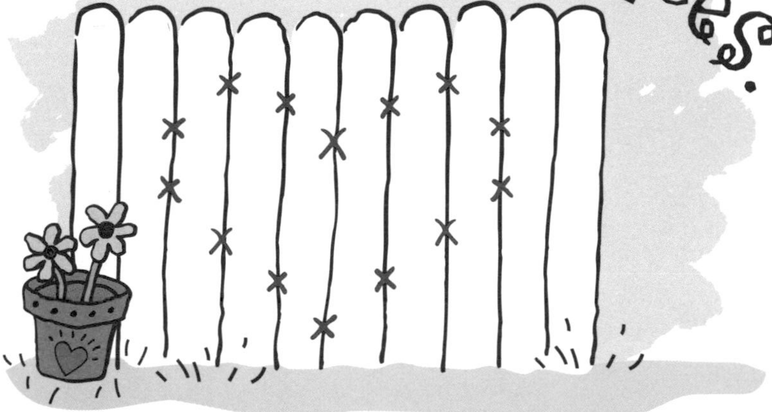

# I'm glad I found you.

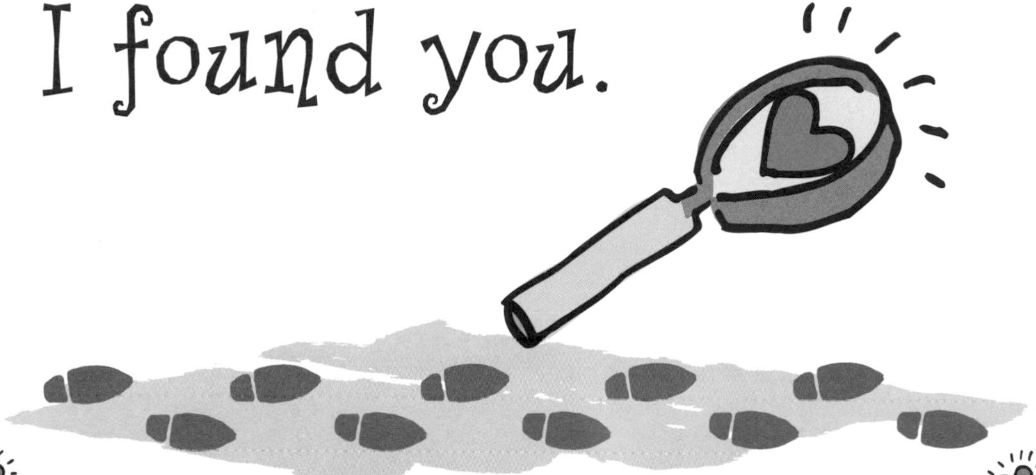

Meet me at _____ for

a little _____

from _____ till _____ !

feel better soon

# There's a hug tucked in here!

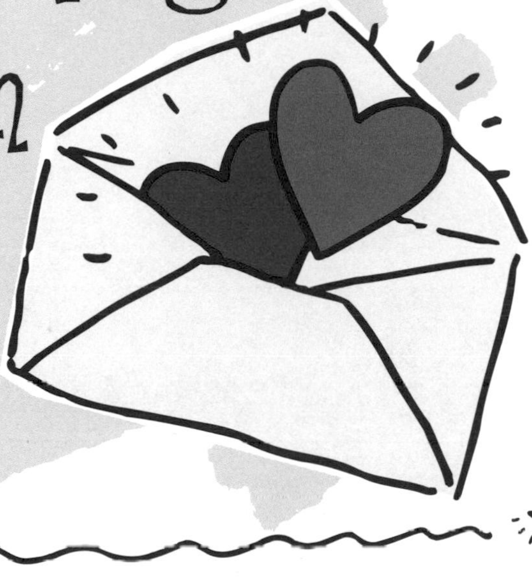

# Thanks for being there for me.

good luck

With love,
from your #1 fan!

missing you

# I just blew you a kiss!